All Around
New York

Mark Stewart

Heinemann Library
Chicago, Illinois

© 2003 Heinemann Library
a division of Reed Elsevier Inc.
Chicago, IL

Customer Service 888-454-2279

Visit our website at www.heinemannlibrary.com

Designed by Heinemann Library
Printed and bound by Lake Book Manufacturing

07 06 05 04 03
10 9 8 7 6 5 4 3 2 1

Library of Congress Cataloging-in-Publication Data
Stewart, Mark.
  All around New York : regions and resources : New York State studies /
Mark Stewart.
    v. cm.
Summary: Provides a look at New York's different geographical regions and the industry and economy of each. Includes bibliographical references (p.) and index.
Contents: An introduction to New York -- New York City and metropolitan area -- Long Island -- The Hudson Valley -- The Catskills -- The Capital-Saratoga area -- The Central-Leatherstocking region -- Northern New York -- The Finger Lakes -- Western New York.
  ISBN 1-4034-0352-X -- ISBN 1-4034-0574-3 (pbk.)
1. New York (State)--Geography--Juvenile literature. 2.Regionalism--New York (State)--Juvenile literature. [1. New York (State)--Geography.] I. Title.
 F119.3.S747 2003
 974.7--dc21

2002154318

Acknowledgments
The author and publishers are grateful to the following for permission to reproduce copyright material:

Cover photographs by (top, L-R) Rudi Von Briel/Heinemann Library, Rudi Von Briel/Heinemann Library, Gail Mooney/Corbis, Rudi Von Briel/Heinemann Library; (main) Dave G. Hauser/Corbis

Title page (L-R) Bettmann/Corbis, David Muench/Corbis, Gail Mooney/Corbis; contents page, p. 21 NYS Thruway Authority; p. 4 Robert Lifson/Heinemann Library; pp. 5, 7, 8, 9, 12, 45 maps.com/Heinemann Library; p. 10 Reuters NewMedia Inc./Corbis; p. 11 Paul Almasy/Corbis; p. 13T Gail Mooney/Corbis; p. 13B Kevin Fleming/Corbis; p. 15 Kit Kittle/Corbis; pp. 16, 35 George Ostertag; p. 17 Stuart Ramson/AP Wide World Photos; pp. 18, 24, 33 Scott Braut; p. 19T Roger Ressmeyer/Corbis; p. 19B Bettmann/Corbis; pp. 20, 32, 39, 44 David Muench/Corbis; pp. 22, 23T, 26, 30, 34 Rudi Von Briel/Heinemann Library; p. 23B Charles E. Rotkin/Corbis; p. 25 Francis X. Driscoll; p. 27 Lee Snider/Corbis; p. 28 Ruth Smiley/Mohonk Mountain House/AP Wide World Photos; p. 29 David A. Brownell; p. 37 Roman Soumar/Corbis; pp. 38T, 42 H. Armstrong Roberts; p. 38B Lee Snider/Corbis; p. 40 Doug Wilson/Corbis; p. 41 David Ruether Photography

Photo research by Kathy Creech

Special thanks to expert reader Edward H. Knoblauch. Knoblauch has an MA from Syracuse University in American History, is the webmaster for New York History Net (www.nyhistory.com), and was the managing editor of the Encyclopedia of New York State.

Every effort has been made to contact copyright holders of any material reproduced in this book. Any omissions will be rectified in subsequent printings if notice is given to the publisher.

Some words are shown in bold, **like this.** You can find out what they mean by looking in the glossary.

Contents

An Introduction to New York

When people think of New York state, they might picture New York City or the Statue of Liberty. Maybe they would think of towering Niagara Falls, or the city of Buffalo buried deep in snow. All of these thoughts would be correct. New York is an amazingly **varied** state. It has ocean beaches and rugged peaks. It has dairy farms and skyscrapers. From its **natural resources** to its many businesses, and from its **climate** to its cities, New York is one of the most **diverse** places in the United States.

This book covers nine geographic areas in New York: the New York City and Metropolitan area, Long Island, the Hudson Valley, the Catskills, the Capital-Saratoga region, the Central-Leatherstocking region, Northern New York, the Finger Lakes, and Western New York.

* * *

Times Square is one of the most visited areas of New York City. It attracts around 30 million visitors each year.

New York Regions

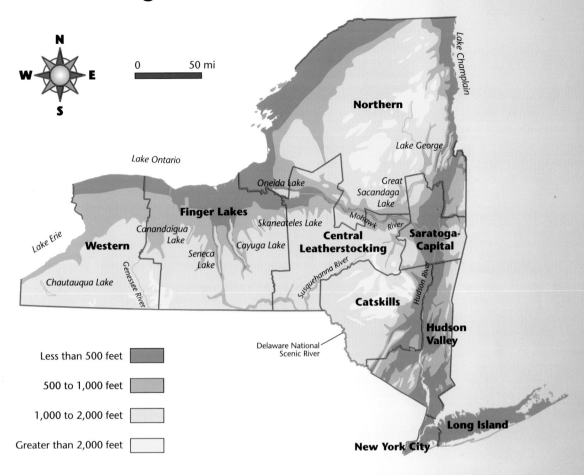

Less than 500 feet

500 to 1,000 feet

1,000 to 2,000 feet

Greater than 2,000 feet

*The nine geographic regions of New York each have a range of **landforms** and **topography.***

New York is located in the northeastern United States. To the north, it is bordered by the Canadian province Quebec and one of the Great Lakes, Lake Ontario. Another of the Great Lakes, Lake Erie, borders New York to the west. The states Pennsylvania and New Jersey border New York to the south. To the east are Vermont, Massachusetts, and Connecticut.

Depending on where you are in the state, New York's climate and precipitation vary greatly. Rainfall varies from 35 to 60 inches per year. Temperatures can also be very different. Near the Atlantic Ocean on the southeast coast of the state, temperatures are more mild than in other parts of New York. This means that in the winter, New York City, which is near the ocean, will probably have rain while Buffalo, in the northern part of the state, will have snow.

To find out more about New York's climate, see the map on page 8.

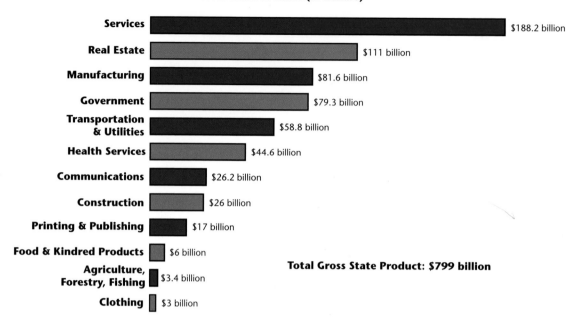

The New York Economy
Its Natural, Capital, and Human Resources
Gross State Product (in dollars)

Services	$188.2 billion
Real Estate	$111 billion
Manufacturing	$81.6 billion
Government	$79.3 billion
Transportation & Utilities	$58.8 billion
Health Services	$44.6 billion
Communications	$26.2 billion
Construction	$26 billion
Printing & Publishing	$17 billion
Food & Kindred Products	$6 billion
Agriculture, Forestry, Fishing	$3.4 billion
Clothing	$3 billion

Total Gross State Product: $799 billion

New York has a wide range of products and services that bring money into the state.

MANUFACTURING

If New York were a country, it would rank as having the ninth largest economy in the world. Its **gross state product** is nearly $800 billion a year. This is the result of all products that are produced in the state of New York each year. New York is home to headquarters for 55 major companies, including IBM, Fisher Price/Mattel, Kraft Foods, and Eastman Kodak.

Those who are familiar only with New York City might be surprised to learn that New York is a major **agricultural** producer. In fact, one-quarter of the state's land is used by almost 40,000 farmers to produce all kinds of fruits, flowers, vegetables, and livestock. More than half of all agricultural production in New York revolves around dairy products. New York ranks third nationwide in dairy production.

NATURAL RESOURCES

In New York's 54,475 square miles, there are many **natural resources.** For example, New York's 7,251 square miles of lakes and rivers, along with its location on the Atlantic coast, provide a huge supply of seafood

New York Resources

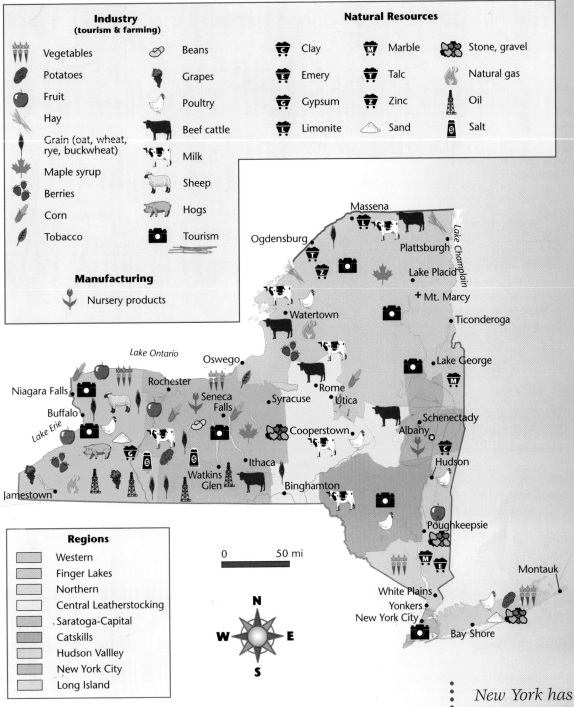

Industry
(tourism & farming)

- Vegetables
- Potatoes
- Fruit
- Hay
- Grain (oat, wheat, rye, buckwheat)
- Maple syrup
- Berries
- Corn
- Tobacco
- Beans
- Grapes
- Poultry
- Beef cattle
- Milk
- Sheep
- Hogs
- Tourism

Manufacturing
- Nursery products

Natural Resources

- Clay
- Emery
- Gypsum
- Limonite
- Marble
- Talc
- Zinc
- Sand
- Stone, gravel
- Natural gas
- Oil
- Salt

Regions
- Western
- Finger Lakes
- Northern
- Central Leatherstocking
- Saratoga-Capital
- Catskills
- Hudson Vallley
- New York City
- Long Island

0   50 mi

N W E S

New York has a wide variety of important resources across all its regions.

and freshwater fish. Water resources also help to draw visitors to New York each year.

New York's mountains are another natural resource. They are useful because the snowfall that melts off them provides fresh water, and their beauty draws

New York Precipitation

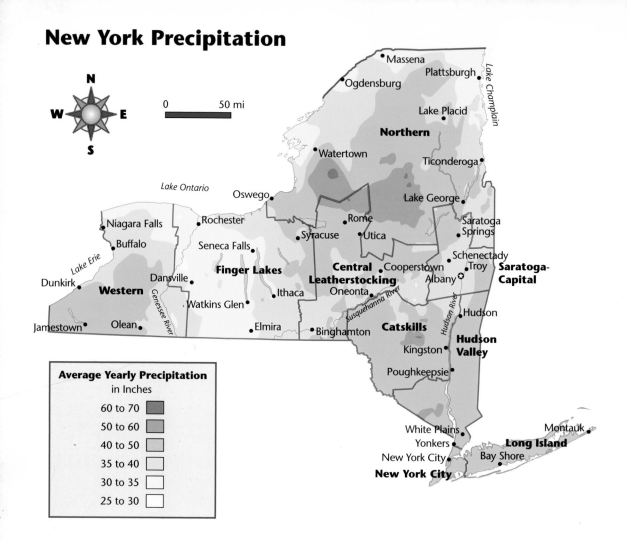

Massena
Plattsburgh
Ogdensburg
Lake Placid
Lake Champlain
Northern
Watertown
Ticonderoga
Lake Ontario
Oswego
Lake George
Rochester
Rome
Saratoga Springs
Niagara Falls
Syracuse
Utica
Buffalo
Seneca Falls
Schenectady
Troy
Saratoga-Capital
Lake Erie
Dunkirk
Dansville
Finger Lakes
Central
Cooperstown
Albany
Western
Ithaca
Leatherstocking
Oneonta
Genesee River
Watkins Glen
Hudson
Jamestown
Olean
Elmira
Binghamton
Susquehanna River
Catskills
Hudson River
Kingston
Hudson Valley
Poughkeepsie
White Plains
Montauk
Yonkers
Long Island
New York City
Bay Shore
New York City

Average Yearly Precipitation
in Inches

60 to 70
50 to 60
40 to 50
35 to 40
30 to 35
25 to 30

0   50 mi

Precipitation is the water that falls to the earth. In New York, the amount of precipitation varies greatly around the state.

visitors from across the state and around the world. New York's highest point is in the Adirondack Mountains, at Mount Marcy. Mount Marcy's peak is 5,344 feet above sea level—that's over a mile high!

TOURISM AND TRAVEL

Attractions such as the Adirondack Mountains, Niagara Falls, the Statue of Liberty, and Long Island beaches bring many visitors to New York each year. New York is the third most visited state, after California and Florida. New York's **diverse** population is another of its great resources. Perhaps that is why New York is a favorite destination for people visiting from other countries.

To help people get around, New York offers almost every kind of transportation. New York is 330 miles long

New York Transportation

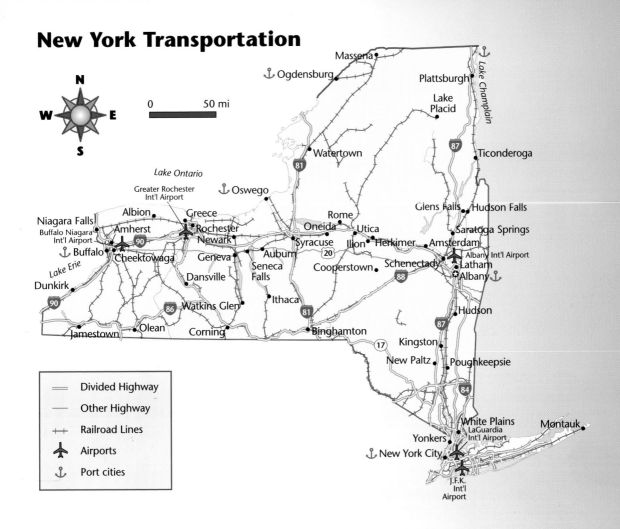

Legend:
- ══ Divided Highway
- ── Other Highway
- ┼┼┼ Railroad Lines
- ✈ Airports
- ⚓ Port cities

and 283 miles wide. It has an extensive system of rivers, **canals,** highways, airports, and trains that make it a popular place for travel and trade for the entire country. Because of New York's geography, **climate,** and transportation systems, people in the state have many choices about where to live, visit, and work.

Over nineteen million people live and work all around New York's nine regions. One in ten works in manufacturing. These people make things you can touch with your hands, such as coats, candles, or cars. About one in six New Yorkers has a job in government. One in five work in a trade—they might be a mechanic, a veterinarian, or a house painter. No matter what people do for work in New York, there are all kinds of opportunities in each of its regions.

Transportation routes such as highways, rivers, and railroads have made New York the state that it is today.

New York City and Metropolitan Area

New York City's more than eight million residents live in five **boroughs:** Manhattan, Brooklyn, Queens, the Bronx, and Staten Island. New York City has more people than any other city in the United States. Only eight states in the U.S. have a larger population than the population of New York City.

To find out more about New York's regions, see the map on page 5.

Europeans established New Amsterdam, the first European settlement in New York, on Manhattan Island in the 1600s. Since then, New York City has been a destination for **immigrants** from all over the world. The Statue of Liberty was completed in New York **Harbor** in 1886. It stands as a symbol for the millions of people who have come to America in search of a new life.

The New York Stock Exchange, Federal Hall, and the Federal Reserve Bank help make the skyline of lower Manhattan, which is at the heart of the world financial market.

SERVICES

Many people who immigrated to the United States stayed in New York City's five boroughs, and people are the region's biggest resource today. They create a **diverse** population that gives the city a **culture** like none other. These people have different skills, languages, traditions, and ways of life.

*New York's most visited park, Central Park, is in uptown Manhattan. It has two skating rinks, a zoo, a castle, a merry-go-round, an open-air theater, a boating lake, and a huge **reservoir**.*

The result is a city rich in the arts, communications, finance, and entertainment. There are 20,000 places to eat, 20,000 places to shop, 500 museums and galleries, 250 theaters, and 100 colleges and universities. New York City draws more than 30 million visitors a year.

The places tourists and residents visit employ workers. Most of these workers are in what is called the service **industry.** They work in hotels, in health care facilities, and other places that provide other services to people and businesses. Service industries account for the largest portion of New York's **gross state product.**

To find out more about New York's gross state product, see the graph on page 6.

FINANCE

New York City is home to many banks and large financial companies. More money flows through lower Manhattan than anywhere else on Earth. The banks that are based in New York City help finance businesses all over the United States and around the world. The New York Stock Exchange and American Stock Exchange are based in New York City. Many **real estate** and insurance firms are also headquartered in New York City.

Five Boroughs of New York City

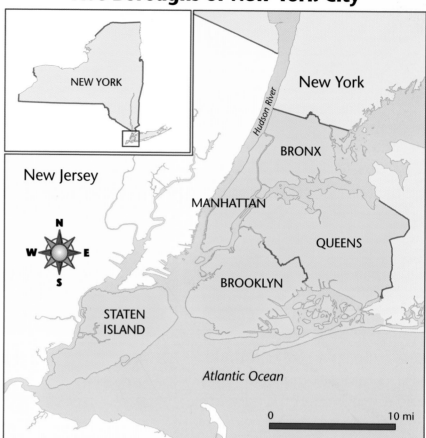

*Except for the Bronx, New York City's five **boroughs** are all located on islands.*

THE ARTS

The arts include things related to the theater, museums, and performances. The arts employ over 130,000 people in New York City. They generate over $11 billion in **revenue** for the area.

Famous theaters on Broadway are in midtown Manhattan. On the Upper West Side of Manhattan are the Lincoln Center for the Performing Arts, the American Museum of Natural History, and Hayden Planetarium. The Metropolitan Museum of Art, the Whitney Museum of American Art, and the Solomon R. Guggenheim Museum are on the Upper East Side.

MANUFACTURING AND INDUSTRY

New York City is among the leading manufacturing centers in the U.S. It has about 17,000 **industrial** plants that employ over 430,000 workers. The most important industries there are publishing and clothing production.

The Brooklyn Bridge, which links the boroughs of Brooklyn and Manhattan, has six lanes of traffic and carries around 145,000 vehicles each day.

The midtown section of Manhattan, where most New Yorkers go to work each day, is where many of the books and magazines you read and much of the advertising you see is created. New York City has more printing plants than any other city in the United States. It creates one-third of all the books published in the U.S. Many media groups have headquarters in New York City, including the three major television networks.

Over 100,000 people in New York City work in the clothing industry. There are factories for all kinds of other products, too, such as paper products, food products, and machinery. These goods are sold through the **wholesale** trade. New York City has the biggest wholesale grocery and dry-goods companies in the U.S. Other goods are sold at department stores and specialty shops, or retailers. They carry all kinds of products, not just those produced in New York City.

Structures from two World's Fairs (1939–1940 and 1964–1965) stand at Flushing Meadows Park in Queens. Both fairs were held on the site, once a city dump.

Building and construction are **industries** that have made New York City into what it is today. Many recognizable buildings and structures add to the city's appeal and help attract visitors. The Empire State Building, the Chrysler Building, Trinity Church, the Brooklyn Bridge, St. Patrick's Cathedral, and Grand Central Station are some popular sites to visit.

Some industries that greatly contributed to New York City's past have changed over the years. For many years, the **borough** of Brooklyn was known for Brooklyn Navy Yards, where countless ships were built and repaired between the Civil War and World War II. The Navy Yards have been shut down for many years, but part

Getting Around

In a city the size of New York, getting around can be a big challenge. In the 1800s, the city built elevated railroad lines above the streets and created horse-drawn trolley lines. To get on and off the island of Manhattan, you had to take a ferry, a type of boat that transports people.

Trolleys and elevated trains were replaced by **subways** starting in 1904. By the 1930s, this system handled up to two million riders a day. Today, it is over 800 miles long! With the arrival of the automobile, horse-drawn carriages gave way to taxis, and buses replaced trolleys. Major highways were built on the east and west sides of Manhattan, as well as in the other boroughs.

Moving between boroughs also got simpler. Starting with the Brooklyn Bridge in 1882, New York City began building bridges and tunnels to handle the ever-increasing amount of traffic in the area. Today, major bridges in the region include the George Washington, Queensborough, Manhattan, Verrazano Narrows, Williamsburgh, Throgs Neck, Whitestone, and Tri-Borough. The Lincoln, Midtown, Brooklyn Battery, and Holland tunnels also serve the city.

of the area has been made into an industrial park for factories, shipbuilding, and warehouses. More recently, filmmakers have started using the large buildings.

TRANSPORTATION

Rail transportation transformed New York City and makes it able to operate to this day. Once rail lines were in place, people who worked on the island of Manhattan could live in the surrounding boroughs. Queens was a quiet farming community until the Long Island Rail Road added a northern line in 1910. Thousands of city residents moved from cramped apartments to small homes. They **commuted** to their offices. Queens today is a major transportation **hub.** It is home to New York City's two major airports: La Guardia and John F. Kennedy.

The Bronx, the only part of New York City attached to the **mainland,** was also a farming community until an elevated railroad line was built. Tens of thousands of new **immigrants** came there for the wide open spaces, and by the early 1900s, the population skyrocketed to nearly 250,000 people. Today, there are over one million.

The **Port** of New York and New Jersey, in New York City, is an important shipping center. It is one of the world's busiest seaports. Around 200,000 people work there. One in every 10 items that comes into the U.S. enters through this New York City port.

We're Surrounded!

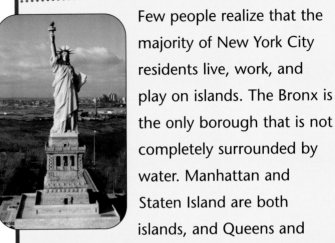

Few people realize that the majority of New York City residents live, work, and play on islands. The Bronx is the only borough that is not completely surrounded by water. Manhattan and Staten Island are both islands, and Queens and Brooklyn make up the western tip of Long Island. There are more than a dozen other islands around the city, including Randalls Island, Governors Island, Ellis Island, and Liberty Island, where the Statue of Liberty was completed in 1886.

Long Island

Long Island stretches 120 miles to the east from New York City along the Atlantic Coast. Long Island is the largest island on the East Coast. More than two and a half million people live there. Many residents on the western part of the island work in New York City, so each weekday, hundreds of thousands of people **commute** by ferry or automobile to work.

To find out more about New York's regions, see the map on page 5.

NATURAL RESOURCES

Before the last **Ice Age,** Long Island was the eastern edge of a long, flat plain that ran from Pennsylvania's Allegheny Mountains to the Atlantic Ocean. A glacier

· ·

The pine barrens are pitch pine and oak tree forests with coastal ponds, red maple swamps, and other wetlands. They extend from central Long Island to the South Fork.

cut it off from the **mainland,** creating the Long Island **Sound,** as well as the many **coves** and **inlets** on the island's North Shore. Beaches stretch from one end of Long Island to the other.

The North Shore also has Long Island's purest supply of drinking water. It became a state forest in the 1990s, and is now a protected area. To the south of the North Shore, **suburbs** give way to large **pine barrens.** The pine barrens account for almost ten percent of Long Island's total land.

ATTRACTIONS

Long Island's location and **landforms,** mainly beaches, make it a popular place to visit. Many people who live in New York City go to the island. Just 25 miles from New York City is Jones

Jones Beach State Park opened to the public on August 4, 1929.

Beach, which attracts thousands of visitors. Further out is Fire Island. One of the top attractions on Fire Island is the beach at Sailors Haven, where you can visit one of the East Coast's few remaining **maritime** forests.

Long Island's North Shore, which overlooks the Long Island Sound, includes many towns and villages where people live and visit. There are many other well-known attractions in this area for people to visit. The Nassau

What's In A Name?

Plenty, if you live on Long Island and know your Algonquin history. The thirteen tribes that originally lived on the island were the Canarsees, Corchauges, Manhassets, Massapeaques, Matinecocks, Merricks, Montauks, Nissequogues, Rockaways, Secatogues, Setaukets, Shinnecocks, and Unkechaugs. It is not hard to find a place on Long Island that takes its name from one of these tribes, including the towns of Manhasset, Massapequa, Merrick, and Quogue, as well as the Canarsie section of Brooklyn and the Rockaway section of Queens.

County Museum of Art, for example, houses Long Island's largest collection of paintings and sculptures. In the town Centerport, a mansion has been turned into a museum and planetarium. President Theodore Roosevelt's summer **estate,** Sagamore, is a popular destination in the region, as is the Roosevelt **Sanctuary,** which has been planted with special trees and vines to attract a wide variety of birds. A **whaling** museum is in nearby Cold Spring **Harbor.**

At the eastern end of Long Island, the land splits into a South Fork and North Fork. The best known part of the South Fork is called the Hamptons. The North Fork is where English settlers first set foot in New York. Today, it is dotted with small towns, farms, and rocky beaches.

In the water between the North and South Forks is Shelter Island. The island is protected from the harsh weather brought on by the Atlantic Ocean by the arms of Long Island's North and South Forks. Manhasset Indians lived here before the island became a **refuge** for Massachusetts **Quakers.** One-third of Shelter Island is the 2,000-acre Mashomack Preserve. This wildlife **habitat** is made up of woodlands, fields, and coastline.

Reachable only by ferry, Shelter Island has been a favorite spot of vacationers for more than 100 years.

INDUSTRY

The land of Long Island is flat and **fertile.** Fish and shellfish are plentiful in its waters. On the South Fork of Long Island is a **port** town called Montauk, which has been called "the world's largest natural fishing pier." It remains today a **thriving,** deep-sea fishing port which brings in fish and shellfish such as lobster, squid, whiting, and tuna. People who fish for a living around Long Island, however, face competition from the 1.7 million people who fish there for sport.

The whaling and ranching **industries** on Long Island grew alongside farming and fishing in the late 1700s. When the Long Island Rail Road was built in the 1850s, Long Island became an important supplier of food to New York City—and remains so to this day. Several crops are grown on Long Island, including grapes, pumpkins, tomatoes, and watermelons.

To find out more about New York's industries, see pages 6–7.

The original purpose of the Long Island Rail Road was to create a route by rail and ferry from New York to Boston.

The Hudson Valley

To find out more about New York's regions, see the map on page 5.

The Hudson Valley stretches from just north of New York City, along the banks of the Hudson River, to the state capital in Albany. Rockland and Westchester—the two counties closest to New York City—are densely populated **suburbs.** Yet despite their population, these areas are still known for the beauty of their river views and rolling hills. To the north and west, there are farms and forests, and the beauty of the Hudson Valley continues.

NATURAL RESOURCES

Historians agree that the Hudson River has been the heart of this region as long as humans have lived here. Actually, most of the Hudson is not a river at all. It is an **estuary** of the Atlantic Ocean, with tides that rise and fall as far north as Albany. This river once formed an important trade route. Ocean-going ships could travel from New York

Bear Mountain State Park, along the Hudson River, is a popular place. Bear Mountain was so-named because the profile of the mountain resembles a bear lying down.

West Point Academy

West Point, on the west bank of the Hudson River, has been an important **landform** since the American Revolution. General George Washington, who moved his own headquarters there, believed West Point to be the best strategic position in America. Troops could see enemies approaching long before they reached the area. This is because West Point stands on a plateau.

On March 16, 1802, the United States Military Academy was founded on this important site. West Point's goal is to produce new officers for the United States Army. Its student body, called the Corps of Cadets, numbers around 4,000 men and women.

A favorite expression at West Point is that "much of the history we teach was made by people we taught." Great military leaders, such as Dwight D. Eisenhower, are among the more than 50,000 graduates of the Military Academy. Countless others, such as the astronaut Edwin E. "Buzz" Aldrin who was part of the first moon landing, have served society in other careers after serving in the United States Army.

City for 150 miles up the Hudson. The Hudson River passes through the Appalachian Mountains.

The gently rolling valleys and mountains south of Albany hide ancient rocks that make up part of the vast Appalachian **Plateau.** To the south, on both sides of the Hudson River, the **terrain** was shaped

The Tappan Zee Bridge carries traffic over the Hudson River. It gets its name from Tappan, *the name of an Algonquin tribe, and* Zee, *the Dutch word for sea.*

Stately homes, such as Franklin Delano Roosevelt's home at Springwood, are abundant in the Hudson Valley region.

by ancient seas. Much of the land north and west of New York City was once part of the floor of the Atlantic Ocean. Clay, used to make bricks and cement, is found in the northern part of the Hudson Valley, while emery, marble, and stone are found further south.

USING RESOURCES

When European settlers first reached the shores of the Hudson, they cleared the enormous forests that lined its banks in order to farm the area. Starting in the early 1800s, these farms supplied much of New York City's food. When the Erie **Canal** was completed in 1825, factories sprang up along the river, making everything from clothing to furniture, much of it shipped westward. At that time, the Hudson was lined with factories, mills, and boatyards. Towns, lighthouses, and stately private residences were common. Most of the farms and factories of the Hudson Valley are silent today.

The Hudson Valley has a **varied climate.** Temperatures are about 18-22°F in the winter and 72°F in summer. Rainfall varies from 40 to more than 44 inches each year. This climate allows farmers to produce a wide range of crops.

Farms in the Hudson Valley are able to grow apple varieties that do not do well elsewhere in the state.

Organic soils provide ideal conditions for growing vegetables and flowers. Some farms even allow people to come and pick their own fruit and vegetables!

The Hudson Valley climate is favorable for growing grapes, too. The grapes are mainly used to make wine. Wineries have been in this region since 1677. There are more than 20 operating wineries in the Hudson Valley today.

In the U.S., only Washington state produces more apples than New York.

The Hudson River, which was once polluted by sewage, has made a great comeback, thanks to a group founded in 1969 called Clearwater. Thousands of old farm houses in the area have also been **restored,** and many of the old mansions are now museums open to the public.

The Storm King Art Center is a 400-acre sculpture park built atop a huge piece of granite in Orange County, just 40 miles north of New York City.

Goshen, a town in the Hudson Valley, was the site of America's most popular harness-racing track. Today, fans can visit its Harness Racing Museum and Hall of Fame.

TRANSPORTATION

Although boats and railroads played a crucial role in the development of the Hudson Valley, the easiest way to get around today is by car. Several major highways and older, more **scenic** roads link smaller towns together. The two sides of the Hudson Valley are connected by a series of bridges.

To find out more about New York's transportation, see the map on page 9.

The towns of Nyack, Piermont, Tarrytown, and Sleepy Hollow are busy **commuter** villages during the week. People built large **estates** and mansions here in the late 1800s as symbols of American wealth and power. Several old estates have been **restored** and made into museums.

The most populous town in the Hudson Valley is White Plains, one of the top **suburban** office and retail centers in the nation. It is considered to be the gateway to both New York City and the New England areas.

In the upper part of the Hudson Valley are Harriman Park and Bear Mountain. Both are popular destinations for city residents looking for outdoor **recreation.**

The Catskills

For people living in **urban** New York City, it is easy to forget that as close as 100 miles to the north lies a vast wilderness of peaks, forests, streams, and waterfalls called the Catskill Mountains. The Catskills are used mainly for recreation but the region provides **natural resources** for farming and forestry, too.

NATURAL RESOURCES

New York's Catskill region includes the Catskill Mountains and the areas to the south and west. This region is northwest of the Hudson Valley. There are about 100 mountains in all, each rising 3,000 to 4,200

To find out more about New York's regions, see the map on page 5.

Only at the region's eastern border, called the Great Wall of Manitou, are there any cliffs in the Catskill Mountains.

feet. The Catskills were thrust upward from an ancient seabed. They once rose more than 5,000 feet, but have since **eroded.** There are almost no **sheer** rock faces.

The area also has narrow valleys with steep walls and smooth floors. Forests climb up the mountain slopes. Maple, oak, pine, and aspen are common trees. Aspen, hemlock, northern white-cedar, and black ash grow on the wetter soils. Other forests in the area might include a mix of beech, birch, and maple trees, or elm and ash trees. Maple syrup is tapped from sugar maple trees.

INDUSTRY

In the 1800s, forestry products produced in this area were shipped down the Hudson River to New York City. **Sawmills** hummed with activity to meet the building needs of the state. The **tanning industry** flourished. The town of Prattsville was a **planned community,** built to house workers at the **tannery** of Zadock Pratt, which tanned over a million hides during the 1800s.

· ·

People come to the Catskills from all over the world for its trout fishing. In fact, the Catskills town of Roscoe, where fly-fishing started, calls itself Trout Town U.S.A.

A church overlooks the graves of original French settlers of New Paltz, one of the two main towns in the Catskills.

At that time, horse saddles and harnesses made from leather were in demand. The animal hides used to make leather were **cured** with tannin, a substance made from the bark of oak or hemlock trees and used for tanning. Millions of hemlocks in the Catskills were cut down for their bark. Pulp from the hemlock trees was taken to mills to be made into paper. Many feared the area would become a **wasteland,** so the state **legislature** passed the Forest Preserve Act in 1885.

Because of the **topography** of the Catskills, soils for growing crops **vary** around the region. Some soils are wet, others are rocky, and some have a mixture of different sizes of rock. Much of the land is used for pasture. Hay and some grain for dairy cattle are grown in the region. Locally, potatoes are an important crop on the **plateaus,** and poultry, fruit, and small crops are produced in the narrow valleys.

ATTRACTIONS

Sports enthusiasts, nature lovers, and vacationers enjoy the wild charms of the Catskills. Fancy resorts and **rustic** lodges were built throughout the region. The hiking trails in the Catskills touch the tops of more than twenty different mountains, and some of the world's best trout streams are located here.

New York's Summer Playground

Wealthy New Yorkers stopped going to the Catskills in the 1930s, and some feared the region would never recover. However, working-class **immigrants** had also been going to the Catskills for almost 50 years. Starting in the 1880s, many families from Central and Eastern Europe rented rooms in simple boarding houses during the summer months.

As these families earned more money, they could afford fancier accommodations, or places to stay. New hotels were built, and some of the old ones were redone. The "new" Catskills reached their peak of popularity between the 1930s and 1950s. By the 1950s, two dozen different **ethnic** groups called some part of the Catskills their own. For many, spending a week or two in one of these areas was as close as they would ever get to their homelands.

The State University of New York in New Paltz is in a historic area with many buildings that date back to the earliest European settlers. The town of Kingston offers a **maritime** museum, several historic ships, and the biggest lighthouse on the river.

As travelers venture west into the Catskills, they are likely to visit the village of Woodstock, created over a hundred years ago as a place where people gather to create art. Today, it bustles with tourist activity, especially on summer and fall weekends. Hunter Mountain ski resort dominates the northern Catskills. In warmer weather, hikers might stay there while they explore nearby trails.

Visitors to the Catskills might stay at the Mohonk Mountain House, a huge lodge built in the 1870s.

The Capital-Saratoga Region

The Capital-Saratoga region might be called the **hub** of **upstate** New York. Home to Albany, the state capital, and historic Saratoga, it is the link between New York City, Boston, Montreal, and central New York state.

NATURAL RESOURCES

This region is located midway up the eastern border of New York state. Its land has sections of the **fertile** Hudson and Mohawk river valleys, as well as portions of the state's two major mountain ranges, the Adirondacks and the Catskills.

To find out more about New York's regions, see the map on page 5.

*In 1918, a government project widened and lengthened the state's existing **canal** system. The New York State Canal System is the country's largest water system today.*

In 1864, the Saratoga Race Course opened. It is the oldest thoroughbred racetrack in the United States.

The famous waters at Saratoga Springs **seep** upward from an ancient sea trapped under limestone and shale. In the early 1800s, the first hotels were built in the area, and what was wilderness became known as Queen of the **Spas.** Fancy balls, concerts, and horse racing were offered to visitors. The resort lost its popularity in the 1900s, but many of the buildings have been preserved. Today, people visit museums in and araound Saratoga dedicated to horse racing, history, and dance.

INDUSTRY

The Capital-Saratoga Region has attracted many new distribution and warehousing centers. These centers use the region's excellent transportation systems to

In 1958, Governor Nelson Rockefeller decided to create the "most spectacularly beautiful seat of government in the world." The result was Albany's Empire Plaza, with several government and **cultural** buildings.

Transportation Center

Albany was at the Erie **Canal's** eastern end, and for decades, the city served as one of the nation's most important transportation centers. After railroads began crisscrossing New York in the 1830s, they also linked New York's cities to Boston, Montreal, and Chicago.

The Thomas E. Dewey Thruway opened in 1955. This highway runs from New York City to the Pennsylvania border. It links the cities of Albany, Utica, Syracuse, Rochester, and Buffalo. It joins with turnpikes leading to Connecticut, Massachusetts, New Jersey, and other places. Its 641-mile route follows the paths originally used by New York's early European settlers.

send goods to market. As state capital, Albany, on the Hudson River, has many government jobs. It is a leading employer in the area.

Located along the Hudson River, Troy was a major center for **industry** in the 1800s. It was the home of the detachable shirt collar, stove manufacturers, textile mills, bell manufacturers, iron and steel centers, and more. Even Samuel Wilson, better known as Uncle Sam, lived and worked in Troy.

To find out more about New York's transportation, see the map on page 9.

Close to 10 percent of all non-farming jobs in the region are in manufacturing, with General Electric Company as a major employer. The region is also one of the state's **high-tech** centers, with several research institutions.

Agriculture is important to the region, especially dairy farming and nursery products. There are many acres devoted to growing hay and seeds. But the mostly-family farms are threatened by the growth of cities. Local people are working hard to protect the farmland, so people can enjoy what the land produces, as well as the scenery it creates.

The Central-Leatherstocking Region

The land west of Albany, fanning out along the Mohawk River, is called the Central-Leatherstocking region. It gets its name from its central location within the state, and from the leather leggings that English settlers in the Mohawk River Valley wore in the 1700s.

To find out more about New York's regions, see the map on page 5.

NATURAL RESOURCES

The gentle roll of the land and the four major rivers that flow through this area—the Mohawk, Delaware, Susquehanna, and Chenango—have attracted people for

* *

The Mohawk River, which extends nearly all the way to the Great Lakes, was a main water highway through the region for early residents of New York.

32

many years. The area has distinct seasons and a **temperate climate.**

INDUSTRY

The Erie **Canal** brought growth to the region when it opened in 1825. Farmers could ship produce to New York City, and manufacturers in the towns were able to meet the needs of people out west who wanted to buy their goods. Utica had some of the country's best knitting mills; Rome processed much of

There are six carousels in and around Binghamton, a town in the Central-Leatherstocking region.

America's brass and copper; and Binghamton made cigars and shoes. Rome and Utica are still producers of machinery and metals such as nickel.

The fortunes of the Central-Leatherstocking region went downhill in the 1900s. Many of the products made there were no longer needed, or were being manufactured in other places for a cheaper price. As factories closed, many people moved away. Today, Binghamton is home to one of the nation's oldest zoos, Ross Park. It is also the birthplace of the International Business Machine Corporation, better known as IBM. Many other **high-tech** companies have sprung up in the region, too.

At the western edge of the region, right in the center of the state, is Syracuse, the fourth-largest city in New York. Syracuse is the home of a large **pharmaceutical** company, as well as Niagara-Mohawk Power and Syracuse University. The university is a large employer, as are the metals, machinery, and paper **industries.**

Play Ball!

Baseball fans love the Central-Leatherstocking town of Cooperstown, home of the National Baseball Hall of Fame and Museum. Three floors and 50,000 square feet of exhibit space bring baseball's past to life.

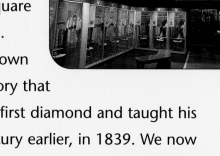

The Hall of Fame opened in 1939. Cooperstown was selected as its location based on the old story that Abner Doubleday, an Army officer, laid out the first diamond and taught his men how to play ball in Cooperstown one century earlier, in 1839. We now know that Doubleday did not invent baseball, but the Hall of Fame still stands in this city.

To find out more about New York's transportation, see the map on page 9.

TRANSPORTATION

The dirt highway leading west from Albany, later named the Cherry Valley Turnpike, was used by thousands of settlers as they passed through the region after the American Revolution. Today, Route 20 traces its path along the main sights of the Central-Leatherstocking region.

ATTRACTIONS

In Rome, the most popular attraction is Fort Stanwix, an American Revolution battle-site. A few miles away is the Erie **Canal** Village, perhaps the state's best re-creation of what life was like along the canal in the 1800s. Young visitors to Utica might head for the zoo or children's museum, while adults are drawn to the Munson-Williams-Proctor Institute, which combines a museum, art school, and performing arts center.

Refugee City

The town of Utica has encouraged **refugees** to move there. Today, it is home to one of the largest concentrations of refugees in the United States. Twenty-four countries are represented, with the largest groups from Bosnia, Vietnam, and the former Soviet Union.

Northern New York

In 1837, a natural history survey of the Adirondack Mountains was conducted. Artist Charles Cromwell Ingham's paintings from this exploration astonished New Yorkers. Most had no idea this towering wilderness existed in their own state.

NATURAL RESOURCES

The northern part of New York state begins just north of Saratoga Springs and stretches up through the

To find out more about New York's regions, see the map on page 5.

• •

Mount Marcy, the tallest mountain in New York, is also known as Tahawus, Cloudsplitter, and High Peak of Essex. It stands 5,344 feet above sea level—over a mile high.

Adirondack Mountains to the Canadian border and the St. Lawrence River. This region covers almost one-third of the entire state.

The Adirondacks were created ten million years ago. The Adirondacks are taller than the older Catskills to the south. Many people assume the Adirondacks and Catskills are part of the same range, but the Adirondacks are actually part of the Canadian Shield. More than 31,000 miles of rivers and streams in the region branch into the St. Lawrence, Hudson, and Mohawk rivers and Lakes Ontario, Champlain, and Placid.

To the east of the mountains are Lake Champlain and Lake George. Lake Champlain begins in Canada and stretches south for 110 miles along the New York-Vermont border. The Champlain Valley has some of the state's richest farmland. Lake George, a couple of miles away, is 32 miles long. Around 225 islands can be found in Lake George.

To find out more about New York's lakes and rivers, see the map on page 45.

INDUSTRY

Even though it is the smallest in population, the northern part of the state is an important economic

Do You Believe in Miracles?

Despite its tiny size, the village of Lake Placid has had a huge impact on the world of sports. In the 1980 Winter Olympics, held in Lake Placid, the United States hockey team—a group of young players—defeated a team from the Soviet Union that boasted many of the world's best players. The Americans went on to win the Olympic gold medal in one of hockey's most unexpected results ever. The team's victory was called the "Miracle on Ice."

region in New York. Three **industries**—dairy, paper manufacturing, and aluminum products—account for nearly half of all the jobs in the region. Other major industries include **pharmaceuticals,** clothing manufacturing, wood products, and plastics.

Lake George is approximately 32 miles long and is nearly three miles wide. Small communities surround the lake, and each one has its own style and way of life.

In the 1850s, the logging industry established itself in the dense forests in the region, and New York became the nation's largest producer of lumber.

Along the western shore of Lake Champlain is Crown Point. This entire area became a busy industrial center, thanks to the discovery of **iron ore.** Further up the shores of Lake Champlain is the village of Essex, a town once known for its shipbuilding. It features a waterfront park where the Ticonderoga Ferry travels to the state of Vermont.

ATTRACTIONS

Tourism plays a central role in the region's economy, and is a major employer. The Thousand Islands,

There are actually over 1,500 islands in the Thousand Islands of the St. Lawrence River.

Champlain Valley, and Adirondack Park are just a few destinations that attract thousands of visitors each year.

On the western edge of Northern New York, where the St. Lawrence River defines the state's border with Canada, lie the Thousand Islands. Inspired by the castles of Germany, Boldt Castle was constructed 100 years ago on one of the islands by hotel **baron** George Boldt. New York's last one-room schoolhouse, which closed in 1989, is also here.

Adirondack Park is six million acres, more than twice the size of Yellowstone Park. The park is unusual because more than half of it is privately owned, instead of run by the government. This way, it can best benefit the people of New York. More than nine million people explore Adirondack Park each year.

Located between Lake Champlain and Lake George, Fort Ticonderoga ranks among the most visited tourist spots in New York.

When the St. Lawrence Seaway was completed in 1959, it opened 2,300 miles of ocean-going ship lanes in the Great Lakes. The 454-mile Seaway Trail runs along Lake Erie, the Niagara River, Lake Ontario and the St. Lawrence River. It is the longest national **recreation** trail in the country. A section of the trail that borders the Thousand Islands area features more parks and beaches than any other part of the state.

The Finger Lakes

In the region west of the Mohawk Valley and south of Lake Ontario lies New York's famous Finger Lakes. Ten long, narrow lakes stretch from north to south in this part of the state.

NATURAL RESOURCES

The natural beauty of the Finger Lakes region makes it a favorite of vacationers. There are many lakes, rivers, and waterfalls. Many people especially like Watkins Glen, a high-walled **gorge** at the end of Seneca Lake. At 634 feet, Seneca Lake is one of the deepest bodies of water in the United States. Glen Creek rushes through the two-mile gorge, splashing down nineteen waterfalls. The one-and-a-half-mile Gorge Trail twists past deep tunnels and caves, over natural bridges, and up and down stone staircases.

To find out more about New York's regions, see the map on page 5.

The Principal Finger Lakes

- Canandaigua
- Keuka
- Seneca
- Cayuga
- Owasco
- Skaneateles
- Otisco

At Watkins Glen, Glen Creek drops 400 feet into a great gorge, past 200-foot cliffs, creating 19 waterfalls.

Rochester offers many attractions such as the Strong Museum, the International Museum of Photography, Highland Park, and the Rochester Museum and Science Center.

INDUSTRY

The Erie **Canal** brought many settlers and much **prosperity** to this region in the 1820s through the 1840s. In the canal **port** cities of Rochester, Elmira, Auburn, and Seneca Falls, factories used the power of water to manufacture and ship all types of goods. The fruit and dairy products produced by farmers, and shipped by **barge** both east and west, made the Finger Lakes one of America's most important **agricultural** regions. By the end of the 1800s, railroads replaced barges as the best way to ship goods.

Although the factories of Rochester and Elmira still manufacture products, most of the Finger Lakes towns returned to farming. The lakes create a warm, humid **microclimate** that is perfect for certain crops: grapes, apples, cherries, and many kinds of vegetables grow very easily here. Also, the region has many dairy farms in its grassy valleys.

The Finger Lakes town of Corning has been a world power in the glass business for nearly 150 years. First known for manufacturing railroad signals, thermometers, and light bulbs, Corning is now a leader in the

fiber optic technology that has become necessary for fast-moving computer networks. A glass museum helps makes Corning the third biggest tourist stop in the state, behind New York City and Niagara Falls.

New York's third largest city, Rochester, is home to well known companies such as Xerox, Eastman Kodak, and Bausch & Lomb. When many of the state's cities began to decay in the 1960s, Rochester survived because of the jobs these photographic and eyewear companies provided. George Eastman, the founder of the Kodak company, gave away tens of millions of dollars during his lifetime—almost all of which went toward the development of the city of Rochester.

ATTRACTIONS

Other interesting cities in the Finger Lakes region are Auburn, Seneca Falls, and Ithaca. Harriet Tubman, conductor for the **Underground Railroad,** and William Seward, who purchased Alaska from Russia in 1867, both called Auburn their home. Seneca Falls was the home of activist Elizabeth Cady Stanton, a woman who lived during the 1800s who fought for equal rights for women in the United States and throughout the world.

At the southern end of Cayuga Lake is Ithaca, home to Cornell University. Founded in 1865, it was open to everyone, regardless of race, gender, wealth, or religion.

Western New York

A thriving industrial center, Western New York is one of the major commercial **hubs** in the United States. The region provides a vital link between Midwestern, Canadian, and Eastern U.S. markets.

To find out more about New York's regions, see the map on page 5.

Natural Resources

To those not familiar with the area, Western New York may not seem like a part of New York at all. Everything from the bean crops growing on its gentle **terrain** to the easy manner of its people are a reminder that it is actually closer to the Midwest than to the Hudson River or Atlantic Ocean. The Great Lakes Plain is the name of the lowland region that covers much of Western New York. The land is flat, rich, and **fertile.**

Buffalo is the commercial, political, and entertainment hub of the eight counties that make up Western New York state. It is home to nearly 1.6 million people.

No Buffaloes in Buffalo?

Has anyone ever seen an actual buffalo in Buffalo? Not unless they saw it in the Buffalo Zoological Gardens. This is because the city's name has nothing to do with the animal. The theory is that in the 1600s, French trappers called the Niagara River *beau fleuve*, or beautiful river. When English-speaking settlers arrived they kept the name, but changed it ever so slightly to the more familiar "bu–ffalo."

The region's location on two Great Lakes, Erie and Ontario, and on the Canadian border make it an ideal area for a major industrial and commercial center.

INDUSTRY

It wasn't until the Erie **Canal** was finished in 1825 that the region really began to grow. The canal ended in the city of Buffalo, which is located where the Niagara River meets Lake Erie. This turned Buffalo into an important transportation center, because everything being transferred from the canal **barges** to larger lake-going boats had to be moved and stored.

After the Civil War, Buffalo became a major industrial center. Everything from train locomotives to bathtubs were manufactured in Buffalo at that time. The city also became an important railroad crossroads, and grew rich from the cattle and grain trade. In 1873, a railroad line was built to transport coal directly from the mines of western Pennsylvania to Buffalo. Because tons of **iron ore** came by water from the Lake Superior region, Buffalo became one of the world's largest steelmakers.

Competition from foreign companies in the 1960s and 1970s hurt the city's steel business. However, Buffalo bounced back in the 1980s and 1990s, thanks to small manufacturers and **high-tech** companies. Buffalo also became important during this time because trade agreements signed with Canada encouraged companies in the U.S. to do business with their northern neighbors.

Niagara Reservation State Park, created in 1885, is the oldest state park in the country. Twelve million people visit it each year.

As the only major eastern city on the Canadian border, Buffalo benefited from these new business opportunities. Today, many of Buffalo's citizens work to produce metals, motor vehicles, and chemicals. Buffalo also offers lots of **culture**—there are numerous museums, a large historic district, and a popular zoo.

ATTRACTIONS

Just north of Buffalo is New York's most famous natural landmark—Niagara Falls. There are actually three falls—American Falls and Bridal Veil Falls on the U.S. side, and Horseshoe Falls on the Canadian side. They were created when the glaciers from the last **Ice Age** began melting about 12,000 years ago. The water was channeled into the Niagara River, where it tumbled over American Falls and into the **gorge** below.

The power of the water coming down the falls has **eroded** the rock so quickly that today the falls are about seven miles upriver from where they were originally. The water spins mighty **turbines** of a massive power plant five miles downriver.

THE EMPIRE STATE

Each of its nine regions contribute to making New York a **diverse** state. Its wide variety of **industries** support the state's economy, as well as provide **recreation** for its visitors. New York is home to famous landmarks, international businesses, and people from all over the world. It is also called home by people whose ancestors settled the land and established businesses hundreds of years ago. From the high peaks in the wilderness in the north to the bustling streets of New York City, New York state has something to offer everyone.

Map of New York

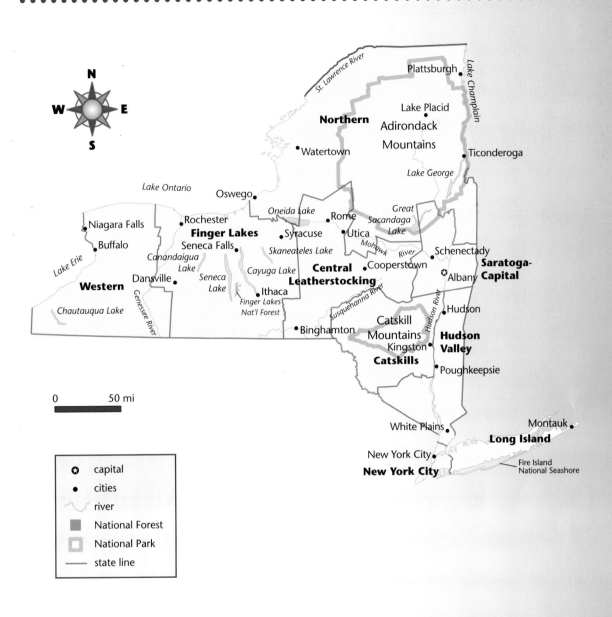

N
W E
S

St. Lawrence River

Plattsburgh

Lake Champlain

Northern

Lake Placid

Adirondack
Mountains

Watertown

Ticonderoga

Lake George

Lake Ontario

Oswego

Rome

Great
Sacandaga
Lake

Niagara Falls

Rochester

Finger Lakes

Syracuse

Utica

Schenectady

Buffalo

Seneca Falls

Skaneateles Lake

Mohawk River

Saratoga-
Capital

Lake Erie

Canandaigua
Lake

Cayuga Lake

Central
Leatherstocking

Cooperstown

Albany

Dansville

Seneca
Lake

Ithaca

Hudson

Western

Finger Lakes
Nat'l Forest

Hudson River

Chautauqua Lake

Genessee River

Binghamton

Susquehanna River

Catskill
Mountains

Hudson
Valley

Kingston

Catskills

Poughkeepsie

0   50 mi

White Plains

Montauk

Long Island

New York City

New York City

Fire Island
National Seashore

Oneida Lake

✪ capital
• cities
⌇ river
▦ National Forest
▢ National Park
— state line

CANADA

Maine

Vermont

New
Hampshire

New York

Massachusetts

Rhode Island

Connecticut

Ohio

Pennsylvania

New
Jersey

Atlantic
Ocean

45

Glossary

agriculture farming

barge broad boat with a flat bottom used on rivers and canals

baron person who has great influence or power

borough one of the five political divisions of New York City; in some states, a self-governing town

canal artificial waterway for boats

climate weather conditions that are usual for a certain area

commute travel back and forth regularly. A person who does this is called a commuter.

cove small sheltered inlet or bay

culture relating to ideas, skills, arts, and a way of life of a certain people at a certain time. Something that has a culture is called cultural.

cure process leather for human use

diverse different from each other

erode wear away by high winds or rushing water

estate fine country house on a large piece of land

estuary place where salt water from the sea meets fresh water of a river

ethnic belonging to a group with a particular culture

fertile bearing crops or vegetation in abundance

fiber optic technology thin, clear fibers of glass or plastic along which light moves

gorge narrow steep-walled canyon

gross state product value of the total amount of goods and services produced by the people in a state during a certain time

habitat place where an animal or plant lives and grows

harbor protected body of water that is a place of safety for ships

high-tech having to do with technology and computers. High-tech is short for the term high-technology.

hub center

Ice Age period of colder climate when much of North America was covered by thick glaciers

immigrant one who moves to another country to settle

industry group of businesses that offer a similar product or service. Things having to do with industry are called industrial.

inlet small or narrow bay

iron ore mineral mined for the iron it contains

landform natural feature of the land surface

legislature government body that makes and changes laws

mainland main part of a state or country

maritime related to the ocean

microclimate weather conditions that are usual for a very small area

natural resource something from nature that can be useful to humans

organic grown with the aim to use natural processes

pharmaceutical having to do with medication

pine barren rare forest type that grows on very dry soils

planned community living area designed around a master plan for buildings, homes, and businesses

plateau broad flat area of high land

port place where ships load and unload cargo

prosperity success in making money

Quaker also the Religious Society of Friends; believe in the personal experience of God in one's life

real estate buying and selling of property

recreation means of refreshing the mind and body

refuge shelter or protection from distress

refugee person who flees from a war or other danger

reservoir place where water is kept for future use

restore bring back to an original state

revenue money which comes in

rustic suitable for the country

sanctuary building for worship or place of safety

sawmill mill or factory with machinery for sawing logs

scenic giving views of natural places

seep flow through a small opening

sheer very steep

sound long stretch of water that often connects two larger bodies of water or forms a channel between an island and the mainland

spa vacation area that has mineral springs

suburb city or town just outside a larger city. Things having to do with a suburb are known as suburban.

subway electric underground railway

temperate mild; not too hot or too cold

tannery place where hides are tanned

tanning process by which an animal hide is tanned

terrain features of the land surface

thriving doing very well

topography rise and fall of land

turbine engine with winglike parts powered by water, steam, or gas

Underground Railroad system of cooperation by antislavery people in the U.S. before 1863 by which runaway slaves were secretly helped to reach freedom

upstate northern part of a state

urban having to do with the city

vary many forms or types

wasteland land that is not fit for crops, often due to overuse

whaling hunting for whales

wholesale sell goods in quantity to those who then sell the goods in shops

More Books to Read

• •

Ball, Jacqueline, et. al. *New York: The Empire State.* Cleveland, Ohio: World Almanac Education, 2002.

Bierman, Carol. *Journey to Ellis Island.* New York: Hyperion Press, 1998.

Cotter, Kristin. *New York.* Danbury, Conn.: Children's Press, 2002.

Heinrichs, Ann, et. al. *New York (America the Beautiful).* Danbury, Conn.: Children's Press, 1999.

Index

About the Author

Mark Stewart was born and raised in New York City. He now lives across the water in New Jersey, where his office overlooks the metropolitan skyline. A graduate of Duke University with a degree in history, Stewart has authored more than 100 nonfiction titles for the school and library market. He and his wife Sarah have two daughters, Mariah and Rachel.